State Arts Policy

Trends and Future Prospects

ulia F. Lowell

Commissioned by

The Wallace Foundation

Supporting ideas.
Sharing solutions.
Expanding opportunities.

AND RESEARCH IN THE ARTS

The research in this report was produced within RAND Education, a division of the RAND Corporation. The research was commissioned by The Wallace Foundation as part of its State Arts Partnerships for Cultural Participation (START) initiative.

Library of Congress Cataloging-in-Publication Data

Lowell, Julia, 1961-
State arts policy : trends and future prospects / Julia F. Lowell.
p. cm.
Includes bibliographical references.
ISBN 978-0-8330-4577-5 (pbk. : alk. paper)
1. Government aid to the arts—United States. 2. Art commissions—United States. 3. U.S. states—Cultural policy. I. Title.

NX740.L683 2008
700.79'73—dc22

2008043624

Cover design by Eileen Delson La Russo

Published 2008 by the RAND Corporation
1776 Main Street, P.O. Box 2138, Santa Monica, CA 90407-2138
1200 South Hayes Street, Arlington, VA 22202-5050
4570 Fifth Avenue, Suite 600, Pittsburgh, PA 15213-2665
RAND URL: http://www.rand.org/
To order RAND documents or to obtain additional information, contact
Distribution Services: Telephone: (310) 451-7002;
Fax: (310) 451-6915; Email: order@rand.org

Preface

State arts agencies (SAAs), key players within the U.S. system of public support for the arts, face growing economic, political, and demographic challenges to the roles and missions they adopted when they were founded in the mid-1960s. This report takes a look at SAA efforts to rethink their roles and their missions, reflecting on what the changes may mean for the direction of state arts policy.

This is the fourth and final report in a series of documents describing a multi-year study of the roles and missions of SAAs. The three earlier RAND reports—*State Arts Agencies 1965–2003: Whose Interests to Serve?* MG-121-WF, 2004; *The Arts and State Governments: At Arm's Length or Arm in Arm?* MG-359-WF, 2006; and *Cultivating Demand for the Arts: Arts Learning, Arts Engagement, and State Arts Policy*, MG-640-WF, 2008—documented shifts in thinking about, respectively, the purposes of public funding for the arts, how closely SAAs should be working with elected officials, and how to cultivate long-term demand for the arts. This fourth report draws on the readings, discussions, and analyses conducted for the three previous reports, as well as other RAND research, to project what the future may hold for SAAs and for state arts policy if current trends and strategies continue.

This document is intended for those interested in where SAAs and state arts policy are headed. However, to the extent that state-level trends and strategies apply nationally and even internationally, it is also intended to spark discussion about where government arts policy overall is headed. It should therefore be of interest to all who care about the future of public funding for the arts, as well.

This report was produced within RAND Education, a division of the RAND Corporation. The research was commissioned by The Wallace Foundation as part of its State Arts Partnerships for Cultural Participation (START) initiative, a program designed to help SAAs develop more-effective strategies for encouraging arts participation in their states. The Wallace Foundation supports the development of knowledge from multiple sources and differing perspectives.

Other RAND Books on the Arts

Cultivating Demand for the Arts: Arts Learning, Arts Engagement, and State Arts Policy (2008)
Laura Zakaras, Julia F. Lowell

Revitalizing Arts Education Through Community-Wide Coordination (2008)
Susan J. Bodilly, Catherine H. Augustine

Arts and Culture in the Metropolis: Strategies for Sustainability (2007)
Kevin F. McCarthy, Elizabeth Heneghan Ondaatje, Jennifer L. Novak

The Arts and State Governments: At Arm's Length or Arm in Arm? (2006)
Julia F. Lowell, Elizabeth Heneghan Ondaatje

A Portrait of the Visual Arts: Meeting the Challenges of a New Era (2005)
Kevin F. McCarthy, Elizabeth Heneghan Ondaatje, Arthur Brooks, Andras Szanto

Gifts of the Muse: Reframing the Debate About the Benefits of the Arts (2004)
Kevin F. McCarthy, Elizabeth Heneghan Ondaatje, Laura Zakaras, Arthur Brooks

Arts Education Partnerships: Lessons Learned from One School District's Experience (2004)
Melissa K. Rowe, Laura Werber Castaneda, Tessa Kaganoff, Abby Robyn

State Arts Agencies, 1965–2003: Whose Interests to Serve? (2004)
Julia F. Lowell

From Celluloid to Cyberspace: The Media Arts and the Changing Arts World (2002)
Kevin F. McCarthy, Elizabeth Heneghan Ondaatje

The Performing Arts in a New Era (2001)
Kevin F. McCarthy, Arthur Brooks, Julia Lowell, Laura Zakaras

A New Framework for Building Participation in the Arts (2001)
Kevin F. McCarthy, Kimberly Jinnett

Contents

Preface ... iii
Figures and Tables ... vii
Summary ... ix
Acknowledgments ... xiii

CHAPTER ONE
Introduction ... 1
Background ... 1
Purpose and Research Approach ... 2
This Report ... 3

CHAPTER TWO
Three Strategies of Forward-Looking SAAs ... 5
Strategy 1: Expanded Mission ... 5
Strategy 2: Closer Ties Between SAA Leaders and State Elected Officials ... 10
Strategy 3: Use of Tools Other Than Grantmaking ... 14

CHAPTER THREE
Conclusions ... 19
Strategic Management ... 19
A Possible Future ... 20

Bibliography ... 25

Figures and Tables

Figure

2.1. Inflation-Adjusted Growth of SAA Legislative Appropriations, State General Fund Expenditures, and Other State Expenditures, 1979–2005.................... 7
2.2. Inflation-Adjusted State and Federal Legislative Appropriations for SAAs and the NEA, 1974–2005.. 11
3.1. SAA Strategies Mapped into Moore's Strategic Triangle........................... 20

Table

2.1. Selection of SAA Services Reported on SAA Websites, for 50 States, 2007...... 16

Summary

In response to growing economic, political, and demographic challenges, a number of state arts agencies (SAAs) are rethinking their missions and their roles. To meet these challenges, they are pursuing three strategies:

1. expanding their missions to include more state residents
2. strengthening their position within state government
3. widening their portfolio of policy tools beyond grantmaking.

We suggest that if these strategies succeed, and other SAAs follow suit, the structure of state arts support—and the types of arts activities that are supported—may look quite different in the future. Specifically, we envisage a system in which SAAs serve primarily to connect networks of individuals and organizations organized around issues relevant to the arts. While SAAs will continue to provide financial resources to selected organizations and individual artists, as much or more of their attention will be spent interacting with members of the various networks: building coalitions of policy advocates, gathering and distributing information, convening groups with similar interests and concerns, and identifying areas of opportunity for artists and arts organizations. Much of their work will center on improving arts education, growing the creative economy, and expanding arts participation.

This conclusion is based on a RAND Corporation study of the changing missions and roles of SAAs. Commissioned by The Wallace Foundation as part of its State Arts Partnerships for Cultural Participation (START) initiative, the study made use of interviews, discussions, quantitative data, and published and unpublished materials conducted and collected between January 2002 and May 2008. This report—the fourth and final one in a series—draws heavily on the three reports published previously as parts of the study: *State Arts Agencies 1965–2003: Whose Interests to Serve?* (2004); *The Arts and State Governments: At Arm's Length or Arm in Arm?* (2006); and *Cultivating Demand for the Arts: Arts Learning, Arts Engagement, and State Arts Policy* (2008), as well as other RAND research in the arts. Examining the strategies that forward-thinking SAAs are employing, it considers what the success or failure of those strategies implies for the infrastructure of U.S. arts support.

The Three Strategies

Strategy 1: Expanded mission. In the past, SAAs considered their primary mission to be the financial support of their states' artists and nonprofit arts organizations. Through a competitive process, they awarded grants to those they considered the best. They thought this approach would benefit state residents as a whole by providing them with more opportunities to participate in high-quality arts.

Over time, however, at least two problems with this approach have emerged. First, relatively few Americans have taken advantage of the participation opportunities that SAAs have helped create. Those that have done so are overwhelmingly white, wealthy, and well educated. Second, the number of arts producers and presenters has expanded dramatically, causing demand for SAA grants to grow much faster than SAAs can meet it. While this increased demand for grants could have translated to stronger and more-effective advocacy for SAA budgets, it has not: In most states, the arts community has provided only erratic support for the SAA, while the general public has been largely indifferent to or unaware of it.

Leaders in a number of SAAs are responding to these problems by taking a more expansive view of their missions. They are focusing their attention—if not yet significant agency resources—on ways to induce a broader cross-section of state residents to participate in the arts. In so doing, they hope to introduce state residents to valuable new experiences, to continue to support artists and arts organizations by boosting their earned income, and to build public support for their agencies by increasing the visibility and reach of their programs.

Strategy 2: Closer ties between SAA leaders and state elected officials. Since SAAs were founded, their staff and board members have typically designed their own programs and made their own decisions about whom and what to support. As part of this process, they have received significant input from the arts community but almost none from state political leaders. This "arm's length" approach to state government has been encouraged by the arts community because it lowers the risk that arts funding will be politicized. State political leaders have also been comfortable remaining at arm's length, for three reasons: It has helped them avoid controversies associated with publicly funded art works; they view SAAs primarily as implementers of federal rather than state programs; and, probably most important, SAA budgets represent only a tiny fraction of state government spending.

Severe political and budgetary difficulties in the 1990s and 2000s, however, have caused both SAA leaders and state officials to rethink their relations, at least in some states. Increasingly, SAA leaders are trying to strengthen those relations through systematic and coordinated public advocacy, more-effective use of their board members' political connections, closer collaboration with other state government agencies, and greater willingness to align their goals and their programs with declared state government priorities. Their objective is to convince state officials that the arts—and their agencies—contribute to important public policy agendas and are highly valued by a large number of state residents.

Strategy 3: Use of tools other than grantmaking. As SAAs try to expand their mission and strengthen their relations with state officials, they are finding that they need a wider range of policy tools. One reason is that their budgets are not large enough to provide grants to an expanded constituency: The nonprofit arts sector is already far too large for SAAs to support through grants, and if SAAs become more serious about supporting other types of institutions, the mismatch between goals and resources will grow that much larger. Another reason is that tools such as convening, matchmaking, advocating, and information gathering are often better suited to achieving statewide goals in areas such as arts education and development of the creative economy, where the ability to form broad-based partnerships and leverage resources is essential.

It is important to note, however, that this strategy does not imply that SAAs will discontinue grantmaking altogether. SAAs tend to see themselves, perhaps correctly, as the only source of funding for certain artists, arts organizations, and activities they view as vital to the healthy cultural life of their states. Their objective for strategy 3, therefore, is to make sure they use all their resources, nonfinancial as well as financial, as efficiently and effectively as possible. This will require a mix of tools, including grants, and the choice of grantees and the mix of grants and non-grants will be different for each state.

A Possible Future

The strategies described above correspond quite closely to strategies identified in the public administration literature as forward looking and value creating. But they represent a change from past practice and may well lead to a redistribution of state arts resources. In the future, we may see SAAs

- increasing their support for individuals and organizations that work in areas aligned with state government priorities, such as youth arts education and development of the creative economy
- intensifying their efforts to expand arts participation
- becoming advocates and information resources for the arts community on such broad policy issues as health insurance and tax treatment of nonprofits
- leveraging their resources by participating in statewide networks of individuals and organizations addressing particular issues
- streamlining their grantmaking processes and reducing their financial support for selected organizations and activities (exactly which organizations and activities will differ by state).

The transition to this possible future entails a certain amount of risk, both for SAAs and for the organizations and activities they now support. Some long-standing grantees may find their SAA grants reduced or eliminated as a result of SAAs' greater emphasis on other objectives; these grantees may no longer be willing to support their SAAs before their state legislatures. Some state officials may withdraw their support for SAAs if investment in the arts fails to produce the kinds of benefits they expect. In some states, the adoption of new roles may require SAAs to undergo large-scale internal reorganizations, and staff and board members may disagree on how best to do this. But in our view, it is inaction that represents the greatest risk of all. Those SAAs that have yet to convince themselves, or their supporters, that significant changes are necessary—or possible—may grow increasingly irrelevant to all but the tiny fraction of their state populations that makes up their immediate grantees.

In fact, we believe that the severity of state fiscal problems in recent years presents a window of opportunity to SAAs. Drastic cuts to SAA budgets could serve as both the excuse and the impetus for making the difficult changes that must be made if the three strategies are to be successful. By adopting a broader view of their missions and using their position within state government to leverage outside resources and influence arts policy, SAAs in the future may be better able to serve artists and arts organizations—and state residents—than they have been in the past.

Acknowledgments

This report reflects contributions from many people who provided RAND with insights, data, background materials, and critical comments on and for the three previous RAND reports published as part of this study. I thank them once again, and refer readers to those reports for their names and affiliations.

Anthony Radich, Executive Director of the Western States Arts Federation, and Philip Horn, Executive Director of the Pennsylvania Council on the Arts, provided thoughtful critiques of an earlier version of this report, as did Ann Stone, Pam Mendels, and Lee Mitgang of The Wallace Foundation, and Sue Bodilly of RAND. Jeri O'Donnell provided her usual expert editing.

Finally, I would like to thank my RAND study team members, Elizabeth Ondaatje, Jennifer Novak, and especially Laura Zakaras, without whom the study could not have been conducted, nor this report written. The findings and recommendations presented in this report, however, are solely my responsibility.

CHAPTER ONE

Introduction

Background

State arts agencies (SAAs) have played a key role within the U.S. system of direct public support for the arts. They have broadened the reach of the federal arts agency, the National Endowment for the Arts (NEA), by implementing its programs at the state level. They have made resources available to the arts at the local level by providing technical assistance, training, programs, and funding to local arts agencies. And they have directly supported a wide variety of arts-related institutions and activities, largely through competitive grant awards to artists, arts organizations, schools, media organizations, other government agencies, and other cultural and community groups throughout their states.

But SAA budgets represent a tiny percentage of state government spending—never much more than one-tenth of one percent—and their work has typically not been seen as relevant to the areas that elected officials identify as high priority: jobs, health care, criminal justice, and education. Historically, SAAs' collaborations with other state government agencies have been limited, and their collaborations with nongrantee organizations in the private sector have been even more limited.[1] Even within the arts community, their impact has been constrained by the small size of their grantmaking budgets relative to the population of potential grantees—and by the tendency among grantees to see them as sources of funding and little else (Lowell and Ondaatje, 2006).[2] Therefore, a number of SAAs, spurred by political and budgetary crises in the 1990s and 2000s, are now reevaluating their missions and their roles within state systems of public support for the arts.

---

1 SAAs have collaborated most often with their state departments of education. While some of these collaborations have lasted for decades, their goals (and outcomes) have typically been modest. One reason is that few state departments of education have prioritized arts education: In many states, the arts education position within the education department is only part time; and in some states, there is no such position at all (RAND interviews; Arts Education Partnership, 2000). As we describe later, however, this has begun to change in recent years.

2 By *arts community*, we mean the artists and organizations that are eligible for SAA grants, plus those that regularly consume SAA-funded arts.

Purpose and Research Approach

This report summarizes findings from a RAND study of SAA roles and missions that evolved out of The Wallace Foundation's State Arts Partnerships for Cultural Participation (START) initiative.[3] START was designed to encourage the development of innovative standards and practices for building local arts participation; RAND was brought in to analyze, document, and disseminate the results. But as a massive fiscal crisis began to unfold in states across the country, state funding of the arts came under attack. The initiative therefore expanded, adding an exploration of possible new roles and responsibilities for SAAs to the original exploration of ways to encourage greater arts participation.

The RAND START study was informed by in-person, telephone, and e-mail interviews and discussions by and among members of the RAND study team and a large number of individuals between January 2002 and December 2007. Other sources of information included historical studies and accounts of the SAAs and the NEA; relevant literatures on public administration and arts education; and published and unpublished data provided by the National Assembly of State Arts Agencies (NASAA), individual SAAs, the NEA, the National Conference of State Legislatures, the National Association of State Budget Officers (NASBO), the U.S. Bureau of the Census, and five national arts service organizations.[4] More-detailed information on study sources can be found in the three RAND reports already released as part of the study: *State Arts Agencies 1965–2003: Whose Interests to Serve?* (2004); *The Arts and State Governments: At Arm's Length or Arm in Arm?* (2006); and *Cultivating Demand for the Arts: Arts Learning, Arts Engagement, and State Arts Policy* (2008). Citations for much of the material presented in this report can be found in these three prior reports; for the sake of brevity, we frequently cite the prior RAND reports rather than all of the original sources.

Because the study looked at 50 organizations across 50 states, its portrayal of the past experience and current behavior of SAAs is necessarily broad brush.[5] SAAs vary widely with respect to, among other things, the size of their budgets, the character of their state arts communities, the strength of their state economies, and the attitudes of state residents toward government support of the arts. Yet as government agencies, all

---

[3] The START initiative, which began in 2001, provided multiyear grants to SAAs located in 13 states: Arizona, California, Connecticut, Kentucky, Massachusetts, Minnesota, Mississippi, Montana, New Jersey, North Carolina, Ohio, South Carolina, and Washington.

[4] Theatre Communications Group, OPERA America, the League of American Orchestras, Dance/USA, and the American Association of Museums.

[5] Our analysis focused on the SAAs in the 50 states. However, this report and the previous reports include some data on the SAAs for six U.S. special jurisdictions: American Samoa, the District of Columbia, Guam, Puerto Rico, the Commonwealth of the Northern Mariana Islands, and the Virgin Islands. We indicate where the data and analysis represent all 56 U.S. states and special jurisdictions.

SAAs must balance responsiveness to their state arts communities with accountability to democratically elected state officials. Further, all SAAs must cope with an America that is growing ever more economically, politically, and culturally complex. This suggests that the strategies now being adopted by some SAAs to deal with these issues—and that are perceived as successful—may eventually be adopted by the other SAAs.

This Report

We describe in this report three of these strategies, providing qualitative and quantitative evidence for each. Our analysis is based on the data we collected, interviews we conducted, and publications we read over the five years of the study, supplemented by additional materials—many Internet-based—collected solely for this report. We then project what the three strategies may mean for state-level arts policy and funding in the future. Our intent is not to make a definitive forecast but, rather, to stimulate a discussion of possibilities.

CHAPTER TWO

Three Strategies of Forward-Looking SAAs

Strategy 1: Expanded Mission

According to their statutory mandates, most SAAs were created to (1) "stimulate and encourage throughout the state the study and presentation of the performing and fine arts and public interest and participation therein"; (2) survey organizations engaged in cultural activities; (3) recommend methods to encourage participation in and appreciation of the state's cultural heritage; (4) encourage freedom of artistic expression.[1] Yet despite this diversity of purpose, SAAs have directed most of their resources to subsidizing the production and presentation of the arts. In the earliest years, they focused on touring works presented by nationally or regionally recognized "high arts" organizations, such as symphony orchestras, art museums, theater companies, and ballet companies. As their budgets grew, they encouraged the growth and development of local artists and arts-producing organizations. They also branched out to include individual artists, artists and arts organizations from various cultural minorities, arts service organizations, community organizations, and schools (Lowell, 2004).[2]

Other than supporting youth arts education, however, SAAs have not devoted many resources to encouraging public interest and participation in the arts.[3] Their mission has been to make high-quality art more widely available to state residents, not to ensure that state residents actually take part in the arts produced and presented. Further, because they believed that meeting the needs of the arts community would also benefit the broader public, their primary constituents were always artists and arts

[1] Drawn from the "Model State Arts Council Act" in Adams, 1966, reprinted in National Research Center of the Arts, 1976, p. 366. As of July 2008, 23 states were still basing their SAA legislation on this model (author's Website review).

[2] As discussed in Lowell, 2004, this "supply side" approach, modeled on the New York State Council on the Arts and the NEA, may well have been the best approach to take at the time. In the mid-1960s, there were relatively few arts organizations outside the major cities.

[3] Historically, support for arts learning has never accounted for more than a small fraction of the value of SAA grantmaking. Between 1987 and 2004, SAAs spent less than 10 percent of their total grantmaking funds on arts instruction, artist residencies, curriculum development, student assessment, and other activities directly related to youth and adult arts learning (Zakaras and Lowell, 2008).

organizations. And while SAAs have used various tools to serve their constituents, their most relied-on tool has been the matching grant. Accordingly, grants are what most artists and arts organizations both want and have come to expect from SAAs.[4]

In recent years, two predominant problems with this view of the SAA mission and constituency have emerged. First, many SAAs have found that their state political leaders (and, arguably, many of the state residents they represent) do not see much value in what SAA grants have helped produce (Radich, 2003; Shugoll Research, 2005). The majority of state residents do not take advantage of the arts opportunities available to them, and the arts do not typically make it onto the list of state policy priorities. When severe fiscal downturns in the early 1990s and 2000s led to increased public scrutiny of state government spending, many SAAs found it difficult to justify their activities to state legislators. In the 1990s, their situation was additionally complicated by a series of highly publicized political attacks on the NEA, which spilled over to the SAA in some states.[5] As a result, the arts have lost ground to other types of state government expenditures since 1989 (see Figure 2.1).[6]

The second problem is that even if the political environment were more positive, simple trends in state revenues and expenditures indicate that SAA budgets are likely to grow sporadically—if at all—for the foreseeable future. On the revenue side, voter resistance to tax increases is strong.[7] On the expenditure side, rapid growth in entitlement programs and federal mandates continues to squeeze discretionary state spending, including spending on the arts (Lowell and Ondaatje, 2006). With their budgets stagnant and the number of artists and arts organizations applying for grants continuing to grow, SAAs are likely to see larger and larger numbers of grant-support demands going unfulfilled, a result likely to have negative consequences for SAAs' political support from the arts community.

In recognition of these political and economic developments, a number of SAAs began to rethink their mission and constituency during the 1990s. In some states, declared missions and goals underwent significant change; in others, an existing mis-

---

4 However, as pointed out by one reader of an early version of this report, SAAs' near total reliance on grants as a tool has not given artists and arts organizations many other options. If a wider range of services were provided, artists and arts organizations might in some cases actually prefer them to grants.

5 We refer here to Congressional attempts to shut down the NEA because of its funding of controversial artworks. See, for example, Kammen, 1996.

6 Adjusted for inflation, state legislative appropriations for SAAs fell by 2.2 percent between 1989 and 2004, while all other types of state government expenditures rose by 3.6 percent. The "other state expenditures" category consists of total state expenditures less general fund expenditures; that is, expenditures out of revenue sources restricted by law for particular governmental functions or activities ("other state funds"), plus bond funds. See National Association of State Budget Officers, 2006. Calculations based on National Assembly of State Arts Agencies, 2000, and U.S. Bureau of the Census, various years.

7 However, as one early reader commented, a number of local governments have managed to set up special tax districts to support the arts and culture. He suggested that perhaps "the public is willing to pay for such things if they know how the money will be spent." See also McCarthy, Ondaatje, and Novak, 2007.

Figure 2.1
Inflation-Adjusted Growth of SAA Legislative Appropriations, State General Fund Expenditures, and Other State Expenditures, 1979–2005

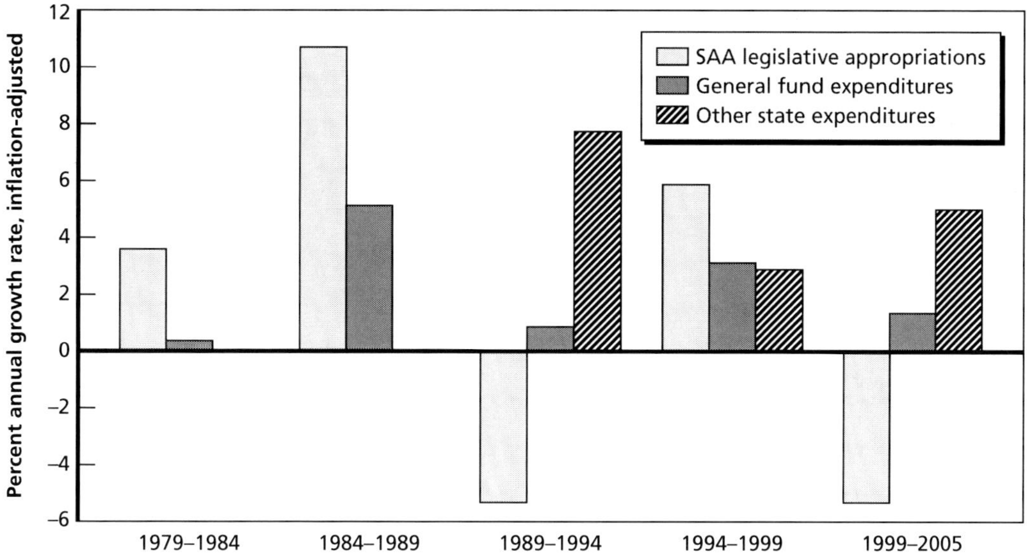

SOURCE: Lowell and Ondaatje, 2006.
RAND *MG817-2.1*

sion was simply reinterpreted. Now, however, SAAs in most if not all states are reevaluating what they do in light of the impact it will have on a broad spectrum of state residents rather than on artists and arts organizations alone. In the words of the Executive Director of the Southern Arts Federation, SAAs are seeking to provide "valuable and transformative arts experiences that impact individuals and communities—and to help participants recognize the value and power of their experiences" (Combs, 2008).

Key to their efforts is building arts participation: State residents cannot have valuable and transformative experiences with art if they are not able or willing to participate in the arts in some way. In the past, SAAs took an "if we build it, they will come" approach, believing that most Americans did not participate simply because they did not have the opportunity. From the 1960s to the 1980s, that approach proved highly successful in getting white, well-educated, middle-class Americans to participate—but it had much less success with other demographic groups (DiMaggio and Useem, 1978; Schuster, 1991; Robinson, 1993). By the 1990s and 2000s, data from the NEA's Survey of Public Participation in the Arts offered evidence of an "ongoing attrition in the audience"—including the white, well-educated, and middle-class—for most of the art forms that were tracked (DiMaggio and Mukhtar, 2004, p. 169). Perhaps most worrying was the finding that fewer than ever young adults (persons age 18 to 24) were visiting art museums, going to the ballet, or attending classical or jazz concerts (Peterson,

2002).[8] In addition to raising concerns about demographic inequalities, these trends pose a political problem for SAAs: To convince political leaders that the arts community is not a special interest group, they must demonstrate that a wide variety of state residents benefit from the arts programs and activities they support.

For these reasons, a majority of SAAs now encourage their grant applicants to formulate strategies for increasing and diversifying local participation in their performances, exhibits, and other events and activities.[9] For example, in 2000–2001, 10 out of the 41 SAAs that offered general operating support (GOS) to arts organizations required their GOS grantees to have instituted some form of community outreach program.[10] In 2007–2008, fully 30 out of the 44 SAAs offering GOS evaluated their applicants on the basis of their efforts to (as the Idaho Commission on the Arts put it) "include and benefit new, underserved, or nontraditional constituencies in [their] activities" (Idaho Commission on the Arts, n.d., p. 2).[11]

Currently, most of these strategies focus on reducing practical barriers to arts participation: inconvenient scheduling, lack of transportation, high ticket prices, lack of childcare, etc. These kinds of barriers are relevant to people who already know they would like to participate in an art form (McCarthy and Jinnett, 2001; McCarthy et al., 2004), but they probably do not explain why organizations such as symphony orchestras and ballet companies have such trouble attracting younger and more ethnically diverse audiences. Here, the barriers are likely to be perceptual rather than practical: These art forms may be viewed as exclusive or elitist, using symbolic languages that young people and ethnic minorities are unfamiliar with and do not see as relevant to their everyday lives. Accordingly, many young people are simply not interested in these art forms, even when participation is made relatively easy and inexpensive for them.

The best way to reduce perceptual barriers to participation, according to many scholars, is to give people the tools they need to understand and value many different forms of art.[12] Ideally, this should occur during the years of kindergarten through high school (the K–12 years), both because children tend to be more open to learning than adults are, and because the vast majority of Americans attend K–12 public schools. However, as discussed by Zakaras and Lowell (2008), the gaps in the support infrastructure for youth arts learning are huge: Few students receive sustained and sequen-

---

[8] However, certain forms of arts participation not tracked by the Survey of Public Participation in the Arts—and not typically supported by SAAs—appear to have increased among young people. See, for example, Tepper and Gao, 2008.

[9] Based on an October 2007 survey of SAA Websites by the author.

[10] Based on unpublished data from NASAA's 2000–2001 Profile Survey, a periodic survey of the leadership, structure and authority, partnerships, and grant distribution policies of all SAAs.

[11] However, according to one of our early readers, many SAA programs specifically designed to serve cultural minorities have vanished.

[12] For a listing of some of these scholars, see Zakaras and Lowell, 2008, Chapter Four.

tial arts instruction, and what they are taught tends to emphasize performance at the expense of other elements of a comprehensive arts education, such as how to interpret works of art within their historical and cultural context.

Realizing this, a number of SAAs are now working with their state education departments and others to develop and implement comprehensive arts content standards in the K–12 public schools. They are also helping members of the arts community coordinate with schools in providing arts learning that reflects those standards. In recent years, their goal for arts education has become quite expansive: To ensure that every child in their state receives a high-quality, comprehensive arts education that will allow and encourage lifelong engagement with the arts. This represents quite a change from 20 years ago, when the SAA approach to youth arts learning was typically limited to exposing young people to the work of professional artists through artist residencies in schools.[13,14] Back then, SAAs did not view comprehensive arts education for every child as an appropriate goal of state arts policy; they saw education as the job of the public school system.

This evolution of SAAs from a narrow to a broad conception of their role in K–12 arts education illustrates how their view of their constituency and mission has expanded. At one time, SAAs focused on individual artists, classrooms, and schools; now, however, many SAAs are involved in statewide efforts to design arts curricula, implement standards, and introduce arts assessments and arts graduation requirements.[15] Additionally, SAAs' growing interest in comprehensive arts education—as opposed to simple arts enrichment—may signal a new emphasis on reducing perceptual, as well as practical, barriers to arts participation.

Having widened their horizons in this way, the SAAs involved in statewide efforts are unlikely to ever look back: If this strategy is successful, they will provide value to a wide variety of state residents—including those that rarely participate in the arts themselves but would like their children to have that option. As described below, an appeal to residents outside the state arts community is much needed if SAAs are to expand their political base of support.

---

[13] It was the NEA that originally designed and funded the Artists-in-Schools residency program first implemented by SAAs in 1969. In many states, it was also the NEA that acted as the catalyst for stronger relations between SAAs and their state departments of education.

[14] See, for example, Backas, 1981, p. 13.

[15] One reader commented that many of these efforts have been in place for 20 years or more and yet have failed to achieve widespread acceptance. Our response is twofold. First, we believe that current efforts are far more focused and far more inclusive than they were in the past. For example, the SAAs in both Rhode Island and New Jersey have pushed hard to include as many stakeholders as possible in efforts not only to develop arts standards and curricula, but also to ensure that public schools have strong incentives to implement them. Second, we believe that because of past efforts, there is a window of opportunity for improving arts education today that did not exist 20 years ago.

Strategy 2: Closer Ties Between SAA Leaders and State Elected Officials

For roughly 20 years after the NEA and most SAAs were established in the 1960s, the NEA was the primary source of SAA funds, policies, and programs.[16] Not until 1974, eight years after grants to SAAs first became available through the NEA's Federal-State Partnership program, did all 50 state legislatures choose to appropriate state money for an SAA; combined state appropriations for the 50 SAAs did not catch up to the federal government's appropriations for the NEA until 1985 (see Figure 2.2).[17] State elected officials tended to view SAAs as extensions of the NEA, conduits for the distribution of federal money and programming rather than homegrown vehicles for stimulating the production and enjoyment of the arts (Lowell, 2004).[18]

The willingness of state elected officials to let the NEA take the lead with SAAs was not all based on fiscal conservatism. A major concern for some officials was their being linked to any controversies that might be associated with publicly funded works of art. At the same time, state arts communities wanted the NEA to take the lead in order to ensure that arts funding decisions would be based on professional values and judgments rather than idiosyncratic political preferences. For these reasons, all 50 SAAs were initially governed by boards of unpaid but politically influential state residents who cared about the arts.[19] Informed by the judgments of paid professional staffs and panels of outside experts, the boards are ultimately responsible for all programming and grantmaking decisions made by SAAs. Together with the executive director, they are also responsible for keeping political leaders informed of SAA needs, goals, and achievements.

The intention in having SAAs governed by unpaid boards whose decision-making is collective was to help SAAs resist any pressure to make funding decisions on political or ideological grounds. In this respect, the arrangement has largely been successful: Elected officials have little input into SAA program design or SAA grantee

---

16 The New York State Council on the Arts, which was founded in 1959, well before the NEA, was a clear exception.

17 States wanting to receive federal arts money were required to form their own arts agencies and make financial commitments to them through legislative appropriations. In theory, the ratio of the state-to-federal-dollar commitment was one-to-one; in most states, however, it remained considerably less than one-to-one for some time.

18 The NEA encouraged SAAs to develop alternative sources of funding, but it too saw them primarily as distribution mechanisms—as well as vital advocates for its budget.

19 In three-quarters of the states, all SAA board members are appointed by the governor; in the remainder, legislators or the directors of the department in which the SAA resides also appoint some of the members. SAA boards in eight states are now advisory only. One SAA, the Vermont Arts Council, is a private, nonprofit membership organization that serves as the state-designated fiscal agent for public arts funds.

Figure 2.2
Inflation-Adjusted State and Federal Legislative Appropriations for SAAs and the NEA, 1974–2005

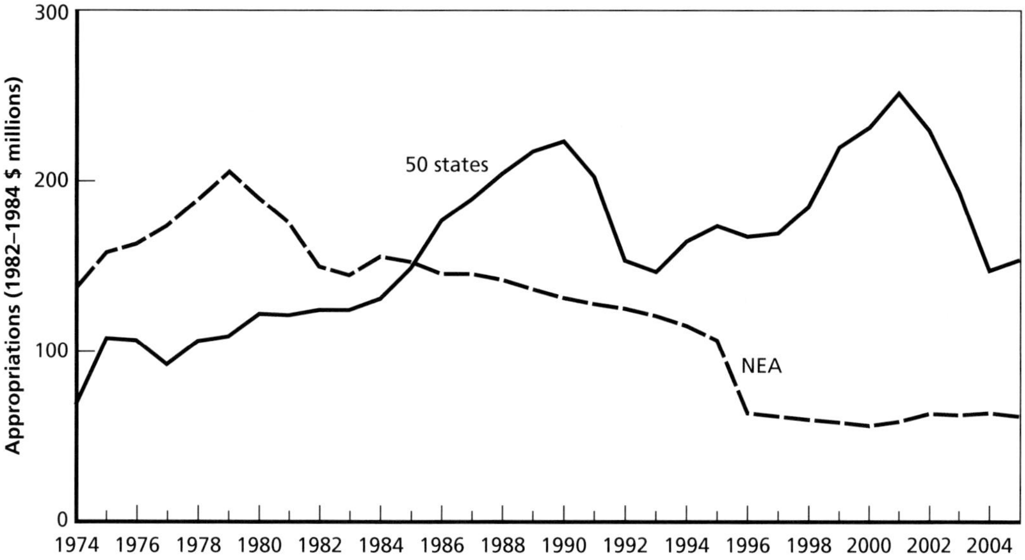

SOURCE: Lowell and Ondaatje, 2006.
RAND *MG817-2.2*

selection.[20] But SAAs' low political profile has also had a downside: Many state legislators do not fully understand what SAAs do, and many view SAA programs as nice to have but not essential to their constituents' well-being. While generally supporting SAAs, they have proved quite willing to sacrifice them when budgets are tight. During the state fiscal crises of the early 2000s, for example, the legislative appropriations for 15 SAAs were cut by more than 20 percent.[21]

The difficult experiences of the early 2000s, and the 1990s before that, have altered the way that many SAAs relate to state officials. One change has been a stepped-up effort to make certain that the views of the arts community are adequately represented at the state house. By requiring grantees to acknowledge state support on promotional materials and at performances and arts events, providing legislators with lists of the grants awarded in their districts, and promoting "arts advocacy" days at the state capitol, SAAs are seeking to ensure the arts are not lost in the clamor of competing interests for state funds. Twenty-nine SAAs now either provide information about arts advocacy

[20] One notable exception to state legislators' generally hands-off approach to SAAs has been the mandating of decentralized grant programs. Such mandates have occurred in a number of states. See Lowell, 2004.

[21] Measured year over year, net of line items, for 2002–2001, 2003–2002, and 2004–2003. The states were Alabama, California, Colorado, Florida, Iowa, Massachusetts, Michigan, Minnesota, Mississippi, Missouri, North Carolina, Oregon, Virginia, Washington, and West Virginia.

techniques on their Websites or link their Websites to state or national arts advocacy Websites that do.[22] Although most of the techniques that SAAs have identified are not new, and neither are their efforts to encourage supporters to use those techniques, SAAs' more systematic and focused approach to those that authorize the resources they need to carry out their work represents a change from past practice.

SAA executive directors are also trying to more effectively exploit an often underused advocacy resource: their boards. SAA board members are typically appointed to their positions because they are politically active. Often they have been significant donors to successful political campaigns. Because of this, they tend to have the ear of elected officials. In the past, however, SAA board members were not always active advocates for the arts; in fact, some SAAs have had trouble just obtaining a quorum at scheduled board meetings (Western State Arts Federation, 2000).[23] SAA executive directors are therefore encouraging their board members to assume more leadership with respect to advocacy. In Arizona, for example, new board members are asked to sign a statement promising to "interpret the organization's work and value to the community" and "further the Commission's goals by speaking with elected officials and participating in advocacy opportunities."[24] In Montana, board members have been heavily involved in efforts to repair the Council's strained relationship with conservative state legislators.

Increasingly, SAAs' advocacy efforts for arts funding and other issues are informed, monitored, and sometimes coordinated by organizations at the national level. For example, the national membership organization for SAAs, NASAA, has been a key participant in efforts to establish national and state arts content standards for K–12 schools and to increase funding for K–12 arts education at the federal and state levels. NASAA, the NEA, and Americans for the Arts, a national arts advocacy and service organization, conduct and sponsor research on the economic, educational, and community benefits of the arts to Americans; report developments in areas of interest to the arts community and SAAs (such as public and private funding trends for cultural organizations, rules governing foreign guest artists and international cultural exchanges, copyright issues, policies governing public art, and tax policies pertaining to artists and nonprofit arts organizations); and spearhead campaigns designed to heighten national visibility for the arts. In this way, SAAs not only learn from each other and from other cultural organizations, but are also able to provide a national perspective on arts issues to state leaders.

---

[22] Based on the author's survey of SAA Websites as of October 2007. Some of the advocacy-oriented information and links specifically target arts education.

[23] A somewhat different problem that has also occurred with some regularity is the board member whose understanding of the SAA's work is filtered through the lens of a particular arts organization.

[24] Quoted by permission from unpublished materials sent to RAND from the Arizona Commission on the Arts in April 2005.

Finally, a key difference in current versus past approaches to state elected officials is that SAA leaders are increasingly looking to link their programs to the declared priorities of governors and legislators. Instead of simply trying to convince officials that the arts experiences made possible with the help of SAAs are of great value to state residents (that is, to persuade officials of the intrinsic benefits of the arts), they are pointing out ways in which the arts can contribute instrumentally to such policy goals as economic growth, youth development, and cohesive communities. Once again, this approach is not entirely new—for many years SAAs have called attention to the economic, educational, and social benefits of the arts to bolster their case for public investment. What is different today is that non-arts considerations are being reflected in new programs designed by SAAs and, in a few cases, even in individual grant allocations within long-standing programs.

For example, as of September 2005, 21 SAAs offered arts-oriented youth development programs designed to help at-risk youth make the transition from adolescence to young adulthood.[25] As of May 2007, a different set of 21 SAAs were involved in creative economy initiatives designed to strengthen their state economies by promoting cultural industries and amenities (NASAA, 2007a). In 2008, "create or retain jobs" and "create or have an impact on cultural tourism opportunities" were among the criteria used by the Michigan Council for Arts and Cultural Affairs to determine grantees in their GOS program for "Anchor Organizations" (Michigan Council for Arts and Cultural Affairs, 2008). The Georgia Council for the Arts used similar criteria to screen applicants to their GOS program (Georgia Council for the Arts, n.d.).[26] It is likely that all of these programs benefit state residents, and they certainly provide much-needed funds to artists and arts organizations. The primary intent of these programs and criteria, however, is not to make it possible for state residents to have meaningful arts experiences, but to use the arts as an instrument for achieving other government objectives.

In sum, a growing number of SAAs are seeking to establish closer ties with their state elected officials. Their efforts include more-systematic and more-coordinated public advocacy, more-effective use of their board members' political connections, and greater willingness to explore how the arts can help achieve the priorities of government officials. As a result of these efforts, SAAs are becoming more integrated into the rest of state government, a trend that is likely to continue and strengthen. The reason was well articulated by Rick Hernandez, former Executive Director of the Texas Arts Commission, who described his motivation for strengthening ties to state officials as

---

[25] At-risk youth are defined as youth exposed to factors that might increase their tendency to engage in problem or delinquent behaviors (Farnum and Schaffer, 1998). The number of SAAs was calculated on the basis of data reported in NASAA, 2005.

[26] In total, five of the 44 states offering GOS in fiscal year (FY) 2007–2008 gave extra weight to applicants that promised economic benefits to the state. Eleven of these states also favored applicants that provided education programs. (Based on a survey of FY 2007–2008 grant guidelines for SAAs in the 50 states.)

follows: "I wanted to anchor the agency in state government because if we did not do that, I believed we would ultimately lose it" (Hernandez, 2003, p. 43).

Strategy 3: Use of Tools Other Than Grantmaking

The third strategy being adopted by forward-looking SAAs is very much a function of the first two: In their efforts to broaden their constituency and mission and to strengthen their relations with state government leaders, SAAs are increasingly relying on tools other than grantmaking to achieve their goals. They are turning to other tools because (1) their grantmaking resources are not sufficient for satisfying the constituents they already have, let alone new ones; and (2) grantmaking is often not the most effective way to achieve the policy goals that SAAs share with state government leaders.

Even if SAAs were given a very large infusion of money, their budgetary situation would prevent them from being able to effectively serve a broader constituency through grants.[27] As it is, SAA grantmaking budgets are too small to have much of an impact on their states' arts communities, which means that they are far too small to have an impact on the entire population of state residents, which strategy 1 requires.[28] For comparison purposes, consider the following: In FY 2004, states spent $173.6 billion, or 35.7 percent of their general fund expenditures, on K–12 education for U.S. school children.[29] Medicaid accounted for 16.9 percent of state general fund expenditures; higher education, 11.9 percent; corrections, 7.0 percent; public assistance, 2.3 percent; and transportation, 0.6 percent (NASBO, 2006).[30] Yet for over 20 years, only a handful of states have ever devoted more than one-tenth of one percent (0.1 percent) of their general fund expenditures to their SAAs; in 2005, the average and median percentage across all states was just 0.05 (Lowell and Ondaatje, 2006).

Given that a large increase in SAA budgets is quite unlikely, SAAs will have to leverage outside resources through partnerships to achieve their goals. This, too, is nothing new: SAAs have long sought out partnerships with other government agencies and private-sector organizations in areas of shared interest. As far back as 1974, 48 out

---

[27] This is not to say that they could not serve their constituency more efficiently and effectively than they do now. According to some observers, the SAA grantmaking process in a number of states is poorly designed and executed (RAND interviews).

[28] For example, state and local governments together accounted for just 4 percent of the revenue of nonprofit performing arts organizations in 1997. Earned income accounted for 59 percent, private contributions from individuals, businesses, and foundations accounted for 29 percent, and the NEA accounted for 1 percent (U.S. Bureau of the Census, 2000).

[29] SAAs receive the bulk of their funding from state general funds. According to NASBO (2006), general funds derive from broad-based taxes and are typically unrestricted in use.

[30] A large proportion of state expenditures on transportation are financed through dedicated bond funds, which are not part of state general funds (NASBO, 2006).

of 50 SAAs had established partnerships with local arts agencies in their states, 38 had partnerships with their state departments of education, and 10 had partnerships with other state cultural agencies or organizations (NEA, 1978). The difference now is in the nature of the partnerships: SAA partnerships are far more collaborative than they were, and they frequently take SAAs beyond the realm of grantmaking.

Take, for example, the area of arts education. In the past, state education departments, SAAs, and the NEA would often jointly provide funding to schools for artist residencies, and SAAs described these artists-in-the-schools programs as "partnerships" with state education departments (NEA, 1978). However, SAAs had full responsibility for administering these programs; there was typically very little involvement by the state education departments—or, for that matter, the schools. These types of arm's-length arrangements suited most SAAs, because they were fearful of being dominated or even fully absorbed by state education departments. They did not want their mission—which they saw as looking after the interests of artists and arts organizations—to become lost in the much larger enterprise of education (RAND interviews). Such arrangements were also fine with most state education departments, which really did not want to be bothered with arts education (Chapman, 1982; Bumgarner, 1994a, 1994b).

More recently, some SAAs have begun using their position at the nexus of state government and the arts community to bring together diverse resources and constituencies in a common purpose. They are establishing new kinds of services and partnerships inside and outside state government, both to influence policies that affect the arts and to strengthen their own position within state government. In the case of arts education, SAAs, NASAA, and the NEA worked closely with a variety of public and private organizations to develop national and state-level K–12 arts content standards. A smaller number of SAAs are continuing this work, building support and devising strategies for implementing the arts standards in schools statewide.[31] These education-oriented partnerships are characterized by a far greater give-and-take among the membership than was previously typical, with all members contributing not only their financial resources to the cause, but also their time and their connections to traditional constituencies.

A second area in which SAAs have established more-collaborative partnerships is the creative economy. This movement, as mentioned above, has caught the attention of at least 21 SAAs—and quite a few governors as well (NASAA, 2007a). In Maine, for example, the governor has established a permanent Creative Economy Council, chaired by the chair of the Maine Arts Commission, to explore ways in which the arts and cultural sector (for-profit, as well as nonprofit) might act as a catalyst for encouraging entrepreneurial activity and creating jobs in some of the poorest areas of the state.

---

[31] See, for example, the discussion of the New Jersey and Rhode Island arts education initiatives in Zakaras and Lowell, 2008.

An important product of the Council has been a creative economy handbook, which offers how-to advice to Maine communities on building creative commerce (Baldacci, 2005). In Louisiana, the lieutenant governor and the Department of Culture, Recreation and Tourism—parent agency of the Louisiana Division of the Arts—originally developed the Cultural Economy Initiative to support the state's artistic assets and preserve its culture. Since the devastating hurricanes of 2005, the initiative has emerged as a tool for rebuilding Louisiana's shattered economy, particularly its tourism industry (NASAA, 2007a).

Conspicuously, grantmaking has played only a peripheral role in most of these arts education and creative economy initiatives, at least as far as SAAs are concerned. Their time, energy, and financial resources have been spent primarily on convening, matchmaking, advocating, advising, and information gathering and disseminating. In the area of arts education, for example, SAA resources have mostly gone toward developing and advocating for new statewide education policies, such as high school graduation requirements in the arts and the implementation of arts content standards. And of the 21 SAAs now involved with some form of creative economy initiative, just 10 have developed specific grant programs designed to support those initiatives. The others are engaged in such areas as zoning of arts and cultural districts, public art planning, convening of cultural economy summits, and statewide identification of cultural assets—none of which involves much in the way of grantmaking (NASAA, 2005).

In fact, as Table 2.1 shows, SAA Websites reveal a number of areas other than arts education and the creative economy in which SAAs are beginning to see themselves as more than simply grantmakers. Some of the services they now provide—for example,

Table 2.1
Selection of SAA Services Reported on SAA Websites, for 50 States, 2007

	SAA Websites Reporting Service	
Service	Number	Percentage
Statewide conferences or workshops	26	52
Advocacy information	29	58
K–12 curriculum guides/content standards	31	62
Business and career management	16	32
Teaching or touring artist registries	40	80
Job listings/calls to artists	37	74
Presenter/venue listings	21	42
Cultural calendars	37	74
Cultural tours or trails	13	26
Artist showcases	26	52
Artist health insurance information	16	32
Reviews/podcasts of arts events	5	10

SOURCE: Reprinted from Zakaras and Lowell, 2008.

business and career management information, job listings, artists' health insurance information—primarily benefit artists and arts organizations but require no decisions about the relative quality of the art. Many others—such as presenter and venue listings, cultural calendars, curated cultural tours and trails, artist showcases, and critical reviews—are intended to make it easier for state residents and visitors to participate in the arts their states have to offer.

Although these types of services, roles, and collaborative partnerships are still unfamiliar territory for many SAA leaders, there is strong interest in exploring them further. At its annual conference for SAA members in December 2007, for instance, NASAA sponsored a "Beyond Grantmaking" workshop that identified a number of reasons for SAAs to diversify away from grantmaking. Paraphrased, these reasons are as follows:

- Expand SAAs' visibility and influence.
- Reach more and different people than grants can reach alone.
- Respond to the evolving and diversifying needs of the arts field.
- Exploit SAAs' comparative advantage in identifying statewide needs and finding policy and programming solutions.
- Maximize the impact of a direct financial investment through training or technical assistance.
- Respond to legislators' expectations that SAAs will be leaders on cultural policy.
- Respond to new concepts of public management.
- Foster independence among grantees.
- Exploit the skills and interests of SAA staff.

The workshop's leaders found that because the two sets of policy tools are associated with different accomplishments, most SAAs will continue to provide both grants and services. They acknowledged, however, that non-grant activities tend to be highly labor intensive and that the competition for time and resources between grants and services is likely to intensify in future (NASAA, 2007b).

CHAPTER THREE

Conclusions

Strategic Management

The vast majority of SAAs were established when voters generally viewed state government spending benignly, state economies were booming, and agreement on what sort of art was deserving of public support was widespread. Today, however, voters demand a high degree of efficiency and responsiveness from public-sector organizations—and have a low tolerance for government spending on activities deemed "nonessential." State budgets are tight, and there are few prospects for relief in the foreseeable future. Further, creative endeavors from a wide variety of cultural communities are now accepted as art, increasing the number of eligible grant seekers and escalating the pressure on highly constrained SAA grantmaking funds.

As SAAs work to convince political leaders that they and the arts should continue to receive public support, a growing number of them will, we believe, pursue the strategies identified above. In fact, it is likely that public arts agencies at all levels of government will implement broadly similar strategies in response to their broadly similar challenges.[1] A useful framework for understanding why comes from the literature on public management: These three strategies map closely into the three points of the "strategic triangle," an analytic framework developed to help managers of public agencies craft "a forward-looking, value-creating strategy to guide the operations of their agencies" (Moore and Moore, 2005, p. 14). Figure 3.1 provides an illustration.

The first of the three strategies corresponds to the compelling mission that Moore (1995) argues a government agency must be able to identify in order to create long-term value for the public. The second corresponds to the need for legitimacy and support from the individuals and institutions that control or influence the distribution of resources to the agency; the third corresponds to the agency's operating capacity, which comprises all the resources, tools, and partners available to help it achieve its goals.

---

1 Local arts agencies may be less likely to implement strategy 3, for at least two reasons. First, there is arguably more financial and political support for grantmaking at the local level than at the state or federal level. Second, there may be more scope for policy partnerships at the state and federal levels than at the local level.

Figure 3.1
SAA Strategies Mapped into Moore's Strategic Triangle

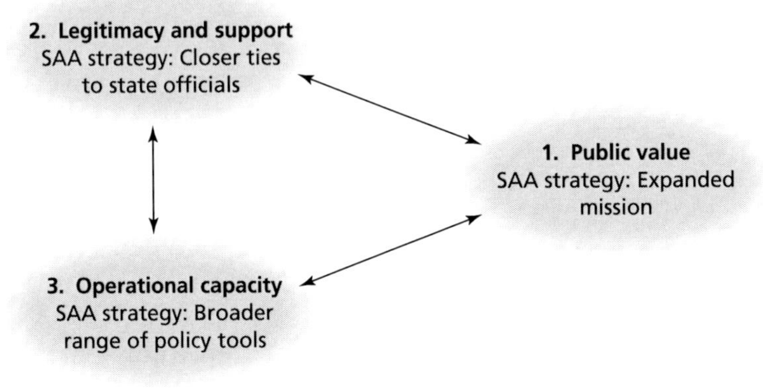

SOURCE: Adapted from Moore and Moore, 2005.
RAND *MG817-3.1*

According to Moore (1995), government agencies serve the public best when all three points of the triangle are addressed—that is, when the mission they choose is seen as highly valuable by state residents, is widely supported by those that control resources, and can be achieved with the resources and methods available to them and to their partners. Our reading of the challenges facing SAAs is that their old mission, supporting artists and arts organizations through grants, no longer addresses these points satisfactorily—that is, not enough state residents see the grantmaking mission as highly valuable, the support for this mission from elected leaders is weak, and the resources for grantmaking are too limited to have much impact on what have become increasingly large and diverse state arts communities.

A Possible Future

What will SAA pursuit of these three strategies mean in terms of the types of arts organizations and activities that state governments support? And what do the strategies imply for how SAAs are likely to support the arts in the future? Based on our observations of what is already happening in some states, as well as a logical extension of the analysis, here are some likely possibilities.

First, state arts policy will focus more on developing the creative economy and improving youth arts education. Although most SAAs are already at least minimally involved in arts-related economic and educational initiatives, in the future these initiatives will probably account for a much larger share of SAA resources, including SAA support for artists and arts organizations. Whether (and, if so, how much) this will change the distribution of SAA grants is not clear, since many current SAA grantees may also be the best suited to helping SAAs achieve arts-related economic and educational objectives. However, it seems likely that at least some redirection of grants will occur, toward individuals and organizations representing economically disadvantaged areas or whose primary mission is education. Further, the new grantees may include for-profit as well as nonprofit entities.

Second, SAAs will develop and expand programs designed to encourage a broad spectrum of state residents to increase their participation in the arts—focusing particularly on the young, those with low incomes, and cultural minorities. The types of activities that SAAs are likely to support in this effort include arts learning in both school and non-school settings, performances and exhibitions by minority artists and arts organizations, and all sorts of efforts by artists and arts organizations to attract new and younger audiences. Some SAAs may decide to support state residents' amateur and commercial arts activities, "celebrating the ways in which people already participate in the arts," as one observer put it (RAND interviews). We may also see greater SAA involvement in efforts to encourage entire communities to participate in the arts. Examples include the joint NEA-SAA Poetry Out Loud recitation program for high school students (which in most states is still restricted to a handful of cities); the Big Read, a program that encourages communities to read and discuss a particular book; and such programs as the Vermont Art Council's 2006 Palettes of Vermont, which convinced more than 6 percent of the state's population to create a visual work of art to share and discuss with others (NEA and Poetry Foundation, 2007; NEA, 2008; Vermont Arts Council, 2006).[2]

Third, future SAAs will become policy advocates and information resources for a variety of issues of daily importance to artists and arts organizations. Among others, these include health insurance, tax policy, affordable housing, affordable workspaces, intellectual property and moral rights, and trade in cultural goods. As noted above, SAAs have access to research and information provided by the NEA, NASAA, and Americans for the Arts, and a number of them already provide information or links to information about these issues on their Websites. We expect SAAs to expand their Websites and to develop greater in-house expertise in the areas that receive the most attention. In this way, they will both provide a service to their arts community constituents at a fairly low cost and ensure representation for the arts in state-level interest group networks that have formed around these issues.

In fact, future SAAs are just as—if not more—likely to be involved in advocacy, coalition building, convening, and gathering and disseminating of arts-related information as they are in grantmaking. This does not mean they will abandon their financial support for artists and arts organizations, but that support will be highly strategic,

---

2 Poetry Out Loud is sponsored by the NEA, the Poetry Foundation, and SAAs; the Big Read is presented by the NEA in partnership with the Institute of Museum and Library Services and Arts Midwest.

and more of it will be leveraged through partnerships with other government and non-government organizations.[3] Many SAAs will also choose to streamline their grantmaking processes in order to stretch their grant dollars further.[4]

What risks may be associated with a transition to this future? Certainly there are some, both for the arts community and for SAAs. One clear risk is that changes in SAA grantmaking will negatively affect current grantees. If those grantees respond by complaining very loudly to state legislators—or if large numbers of them simply fail to support their SAAs at appropriations time—they could well stall the transition, perhaps even prevent it altogether. Therefore, for the transition to be successful, SAAs must convince a substantial number of their grantees that change is necessary, desirable, and inevitable.

Another risk is that SAAs will overemphasize such benefits as job growth or improved rates of high school graduation in justifying arts investments to elected officials and, in consequence, be required to divert funding to programs that promise more of these kinds of benefits, regardless of whether the programs also provide state residents with valuable arts experiences.[5] Related to this is loss of SAA credibility with state government leaders should the promised benefits fail to materialize.

Finally, a third risk lies in the internal changes that SAAs may have to make to successfully transition to this future. Staff members who formerly spent their time soliciting and evaluating grant applications may need to be retrained; board members may have to become more active in strategic planning for the agency; organizational structures may have to be overhauled to accommodate new functions. In some states, the required changes will be dramatic and will almost certainly make some people unhappy. Thus, given the typically somewhat inflexible nature of state employment systems, communication among SAA staff and board members will have to be especially open during the period of change, and the approach taken will need to be highly inclusive.

These risks are real. Yet we believe, for all the reasons discussed above, that change will ultimately prove less risky for SAAs—and for the arts community—than will clinging to a system of arts support developed 40 years ago. It is in SAAs' interests to take the lead in their own reinvention. In the future that we are projecting, SAAs will not necessarily have more money to spend, but they will be in a position to use their money to greater effect. They will reach more state residents, help put the arts on state policy agendas, and play a key role in fostering conditions under which the arts can

---

3 SAA grantmaking is already leveraged through the mechanism of the matching grant, whereby grantees must match government dollars with dollars contributed by private donors, typically at a one-to-one ratio. The extent to which this mechanism actually stimulates new donations is unclear, as shown by Schuster (1989).

4 Some SAAs may follow the example of the Pennsylvania Council on the Arts, which has collapsed its once large and complicated menu of grants for organizations into just three main tracks. Eligibility is determined by budget size and tenure in the system. For more details, see Pennsylvania Council on the Arts, 2005.

5 As we noted earlier, this is already happening in a few states.

thrive. Acting as advocates, matchmakers, conveners, and information resources, they will leverage financial and nonfinancial resources from many different sources, thereby positioning themselves to do more for the arts and for state residents than they could have done through grantmaking alone.

Bibliography

Adams, William Howard, *The Politics of Arts: Forming a State Arts Council*, New York: Arts Councils of America, 1966.

Arts Education Partnership, The John F. Kennedy Center for the Performing Arts, National Assembly of State Arts Agencies, and National Endowment for the Arts, *Strengthening State-Level Arts Education Partnerships*, Washington, D.C.: Arts Education Partnership, 2000.

Backas, James J., *Public Arts Agencies: Toward National Public Policy*, a report based on the proceedings of the Policy Study Group on Federal-State Relationships held at Arlington, Va., July 11–12, 1981, Washington, D.C.: National Assembly of State Arts Agencies, August 1981.

Baldacci, John E., "An Order to Advance Maine's Creative Economy," Executive Order of the Governor of Maine, January 25, 2005. As of September 15, 2008: http://maine.gov/tools/whatsnew/index.php?topic=Gov_Executive_Orders&id=21369&v=Article

Bumgarner, Constance M., "Artists in the Classrooms: The Impact and Consequences of the National Endowment for the Arts' Artist Residency Program on K–12 Education (Part I)," *Arts Education Policy Review*, Vol. 95, January/February 1994a.

Bumgarner, Constance M., "Artists in the Classrooms: The Impact and Consequences of the National Endowment for the Arts' Artist Residency Program on K–12 Education (Part II)," *Arts Education Policy Review*, Vol. 95, March/April 1994b.

Chapman, Laura H., *Instant Art, Instant Culture: The Unspoken Policy for American Schools*, New York: Teachers College Press, 1982.

Combs, Gerri, "From the Executive Director," *SouthArts: Southern Arts Federation Monthly Newsletter*, January 2008.

DiMaggio, Paul J., and Toqir Mukhtar, "Arts Participation as Social Capital in the United States, 1982–2002: Signs of Decline," *Poetics*, Vol. 32, No. 2, April 2004, pp. 169–194.

DiMaggio, Paul J., and Michael Useem, "Social Class and Arts Consumption: The Origins and Consequences of Class Differences in Exposure to the Arts in America," *Theory and Society*, Vol. 5, No. 1, Spring 1978, pp. 141–161.

Farnum, Marlene, and Rebecca Schaffer, *YouthARTS Handbook: Arts Programs for Youth at Risk*, Washington, D.C.: Americans for the Arts, 1998.

Georgia Council for the Arts, *General Operating Support (GOS), Single Year or Year 1: FY2009 Application Instructions*, n.d. As of May 2008: http://www.gaarts.org/documents/GOSSY_Year1ApplicationInstructions.pdf

Hernandez, Rick, "The Texas Perspective," in *Re-Envisioning the State Arts Agency*, proceedings of a symposium held by the Western States Arts Federation, Denver, Colo., October 17–19, 2003, pp. 43–45.

Idaho Commission on the Arts, "General Operating Support," n.d. As of April 2008:
http://www.arts.idaho.gov/grants/operating.aspx

Kammen, Michael, "Culture and the State in America," *Journal of American History*, Vol. 83, December 1996, pp. 791–834. Reprinted in G. Bradford, M. Gary, and G. Wallach, eds., *The Politics of Culture: Policy Perspectives for Individuals, Institutions, and Communities*, New York: The New Press, 2000, pp. 114–140.

Lowell, Julia F., *State Arts Agencies 1965–2003: Whose Interests to Serve?* MG-121-WF, Santa Monica, Calif.: RAND Corporation, 2004. As of September 15, 2008:
http://www.rand.org/pubs/monographs/MG121/

Lowell, Julia F., and Elizabeth Heneghan Ondaatje, *The Arts and State Governments: At Arm's Length or Arm in Arm?* MG-359-WF, Santa Monica, Calif.: RAND Corporation, 2006. As of September 15, 2008:
http://www.rand.org/pubs/monographs/MG359/

McCarthy, Kevin F., and Kimberly Jinnett, *A New Framework for Building Participation in the Arts*, MR-1323-WRDF, Santa Monica, Calif.: RAND Corporation, 2001. As of September 15, 2008:
http://www.rand.org/pubs/monograph_reports/MR1323/

McCarthy, Kevin F., Elizabeth H. Ondaatje, and Jennifer L. Novak, *Arts and Culture in the Metropolis: Strategies for Sustainability*, MG-477-WPF, Santa Monica, Calif.: RAND Corporation, 2007. As of September 15, 2008:
http://www.rand.org/pubs/monographs/MG477/

McCarthy, Kevin F., Elizabeth H. Ondaatje, Laura Zakaras, and Arthur Brooks, *Gifts of the Muse: Reframing the Debate About the Benefits of the Arts*, MG-218-WF, Santa Monica, Calif.: RAND Corporation, 2004. As of September 15, 2008:
http://www.rand.org/pubs/monographs/MG218/

Michigan Council for Arts and Cultural Affairs, *Anchor Organizations Program*, 2008. As of May 2008:
http://www.michigan.gov/documents/hal/mcaca_Anchors_Guidelines_09_231825_7.pdf

Moore, Mark H., *Creating Public Value: Strategic Management in Government*, Cambridge, Mass.: Harvard University Press, 1995.

Moore, Mark H., and Gaylen Williams Moore, *Creating Public Value Through State Arts Agencies*, Minneapolis, Minn.: Arts Midwest, 2005.

National Assembly of State Arts Agencies (NASAA), *State Arts Agency Public Funding Sourcebook 1966–2000*, Washington, D.C.: NASAA, 2000.

National Assembly of State Arts Agencies (NASAA), "States and the Creative Economy," *State Policy Briefs*, Vol. 1, No. 1, 2005.

National Assembly of State Arts Agencies (NASAA), "States Arts Agency Creative Economy Initiatives," NASAA Creative Economy Resource Center, May 2007a. As of September 15, 2008:
http://www.nasaa-arts.org/artworks/creativeeconomy_initiatives.html

National Assembly of State Arts Agencies (NASAA), "Beyond Grantmaking Workshop: Discussion Notes," unpublished background notes for Assembly 2007, Baltimore, Md., December 7, 2007b. As of September 15, 2008, on NASAA member Webpage:
http://www.nasaa-arts.org/nasaanews/2007assembly-proceedings.shtml

National Association of State Budget Officers (NASBO), *State Expenditure Report*, Washington, D.C.: NASBO, 2006.

National Endowment for the Arts (NEA), *State Arts Agencies in 1974: Present and Accounted For*, NEA Research Report No. 8, Washington, D.C.: NEA, April 1978.

National Endowment for the Arts (NEA), "About the Big Read," 2008. As of May 2008:
http://www.neabigread.org/about.php

National Endowment for the Arts (NEA) and Poetry Foundation, "Poetry Out Loud," 2007. As of September 15, 2008:
http://www.poetryoutloud.org/

National Research Center of the Arts, Inc., *Study of State Arts Agencies: A Comprehensive Report*, New York: National Research Center of the Arts, 1976.

Pennsylvania Council on the Arts, *Strategic Plan 2006–2010*, 2005. As of September 15, 2008:
http://pacouncilonthearts.org/docs_upload/Strategic_Plan06-10.pdf

Pennsylvania Council on the Arts, "Funding for Organizations," n.d. As of September 15, 2008:
http://pacouncilonthearts.org/pca.cfm?id=48&level=Second

Peterson, Richard A., *Age and Arts Participation, 1982–1997*, NEA Research Division Report No. 42, Santa Ana, Calif.: Seven Locks Press, 2002.

Radich, Anthony, ed., *Re-Envisioning State Arts Agencies*, proceedings of a symposium held by the Western State Arts Federation, Denver, Colo., October 17–19, 2003.

Robinson, John P., *Arts Participation in America: 1982–1992*, NEA Research Division Report No. 27, Washington, D.C.: NEA, October 1993.

Schuster, J. Mark, "Government Leverage of Private Support," in M. J. Wyszomirski and P. Clubb, eds., *The Cost of Culture*, New York: American Council for the Arts, 1989, pp. 63–97.

Schuster, J. Mark, *The Audience for American Art Museums*, NEA Research Report No. 23, Cabin John, Md.: Seven Locks Press, 1991.

Shugoll Research, "Focus Groups with State Legislators and Legislative Staff," a report on focus groups conducted for the National Assembly of State Arts Agencies and National Conference of State Legislatures, Denver, Colo., and Bethesda, Md., October 2005. As of April 2008 on NASAA member Website:
http://members.nasaa-arts.org/central.shtml

Tepper, Steven J., and Yang Gao, "Engaging Art: What Counts?" in S. J. Tepper and B. Ivey, eds., *Engaging Art: The Next Great Transformation of America's Cultural Life*, New York: Routledge, Taylor and Francis Group, 2008.

U.S. Bureau of the Census, *1997 Economic Census: Arts, Entertainment, and Recreation*, Washington, D.C.: U.S. Bureau of the Census, 2000.

U.S. Bureau of the Census, *Statistical Abstract of the United States*, Washington, D.C.: U.S. Bureau of the Census, various years.

Vermont Arts Council, "Palettes of Vermont," 2006. As of September 15, 2008:
http://www.vermontartscouncil.org/tabid/62/Default.aspx

Western State Arts Federation, *State Arts Agency Governing Boards: A Review of Selected Issues*, Denver, Colo.: Western State Arts Federation, August 2000.

Zakaras, Laura, and Julia F. Lowell, *Cultivating Demand for the Arts: Arts Learning, Arts Engagement, and State Arts Policy*, MG-640-WF, Santa Monica, Calif.: RAND Corporation, 2008. As of September 15, 2008:
http://www.rand.org/pubs/monographs/MG640/